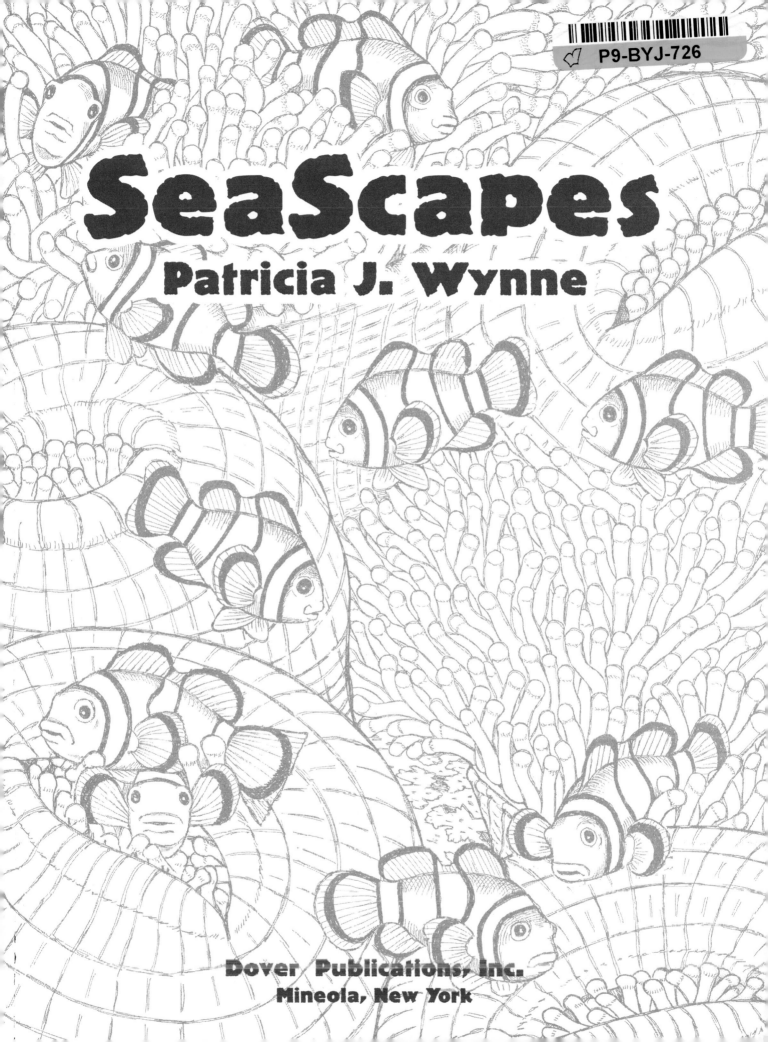

SeaScapes
Patricia J. Wynne

Dover Publications, Inc.
Mineola, New York

Note

The natural beauty of the ocean waters, along with the distinctive shapes, sizes, and colors of its many inhabitants, have often made it the source of inspiration behind great works of art. Here you'll find a group of sea turtles among Elkhorn coral, a basket sponge with brittle stars, clownfish with a strawberry anemone, plus many other scenic illustrations—all inspired by the sea and its interesting residents. The 30 black-and-white images will make a unique project for colorists of all ages. Just add color with crayons, markers, or colored pencils to add your own personal touch to these under-the-sea designs.

Bibliographical Note

SeaScapes, published by Dover Publications, Inc., in 2013, is a republication of the edition originally published by Dover in 2010.

International Standard Book Number
ISBN-13: 978-0-486-49423-4
ISBN-10: 0-486-49423-3

Manufactured in the United States by RR Donnelley
49423310   2015
www.doverpublications.com

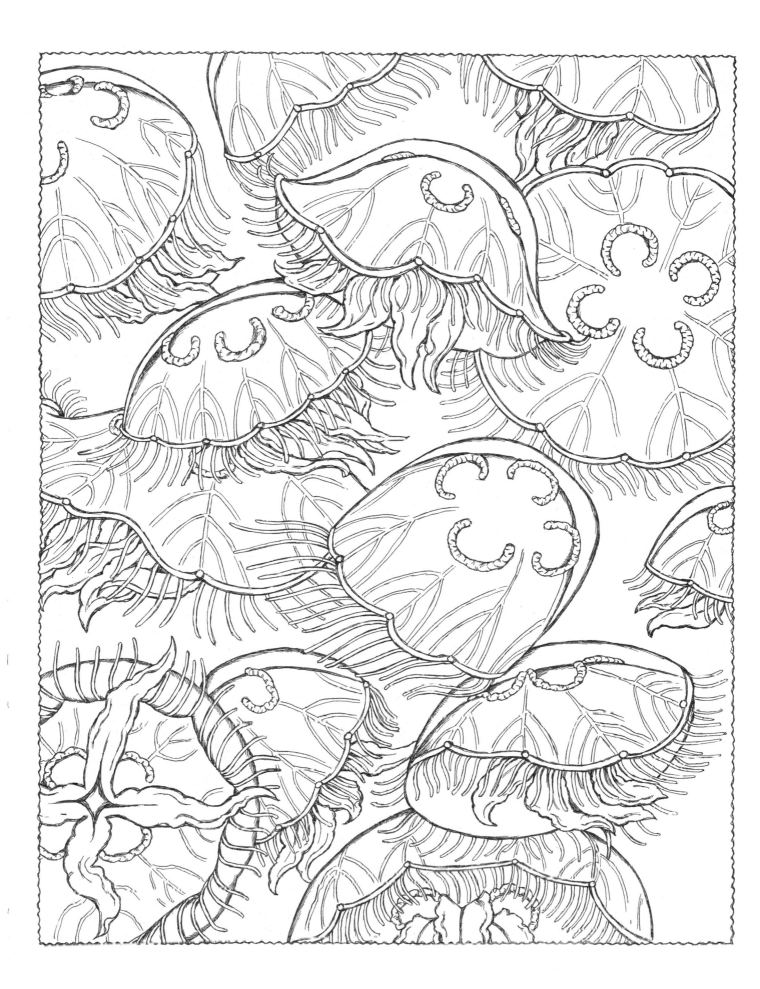

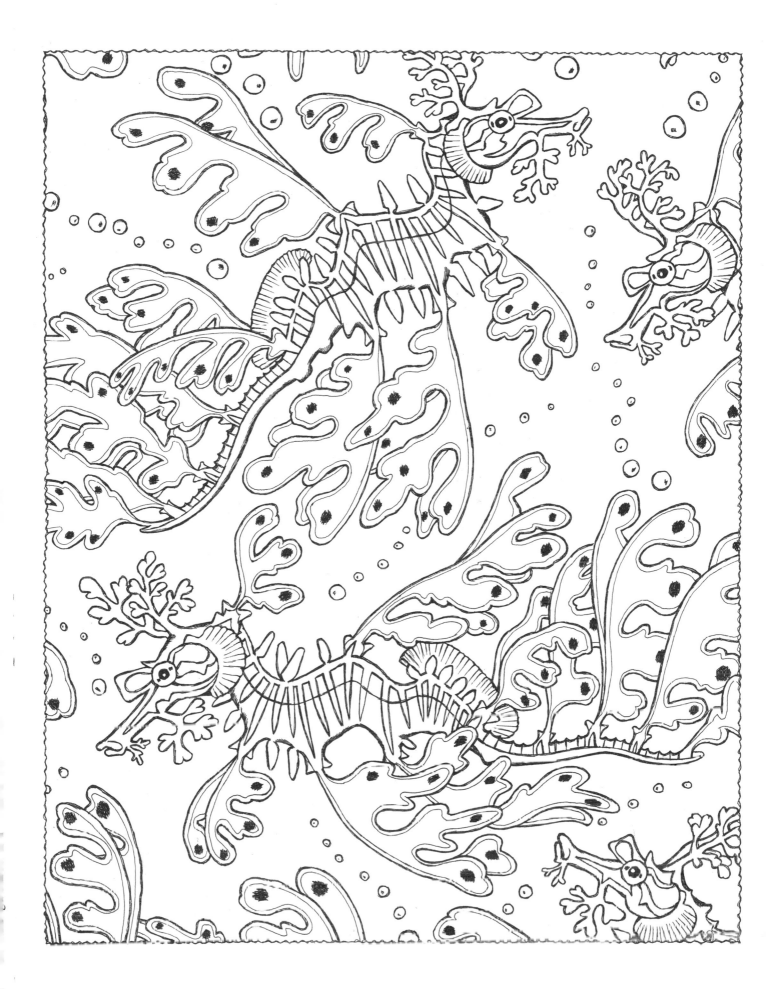

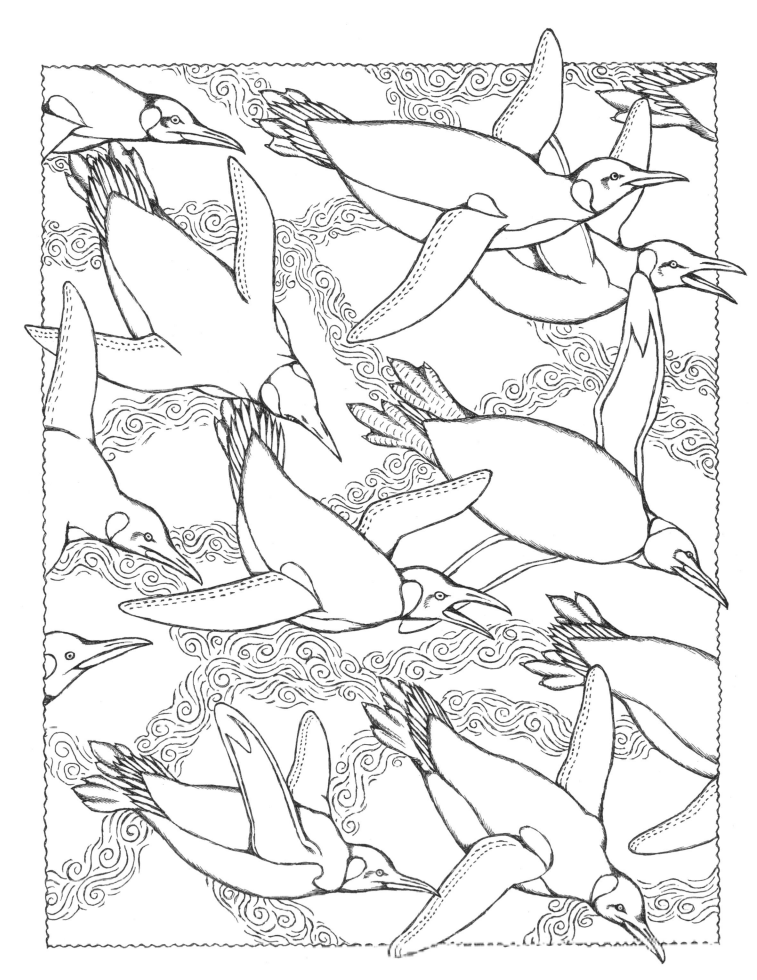

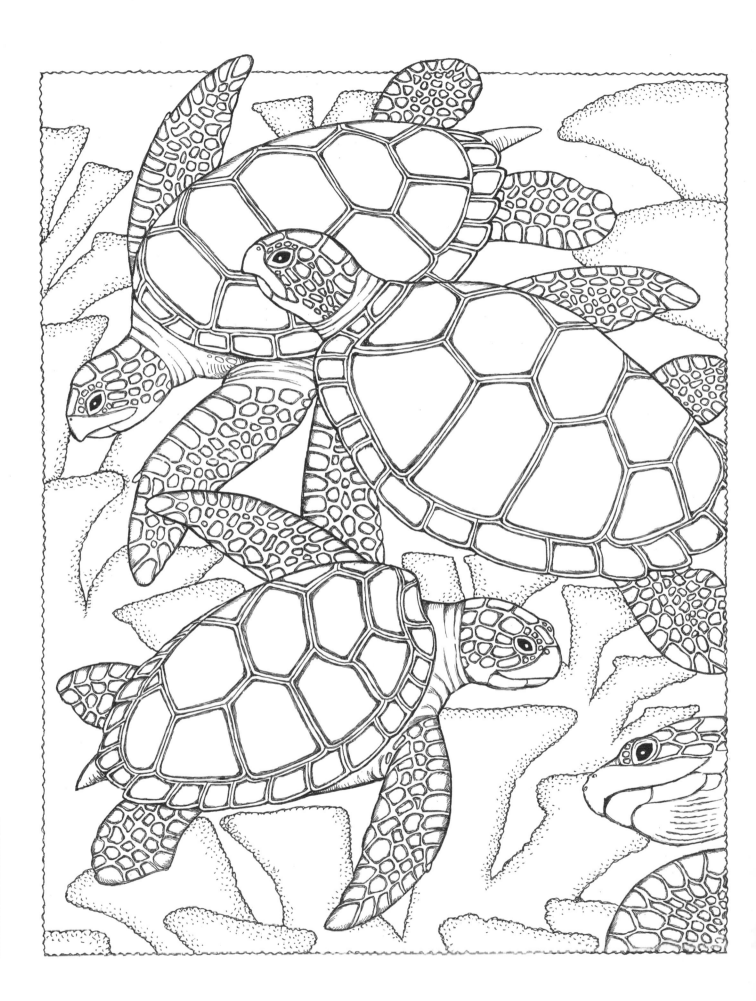

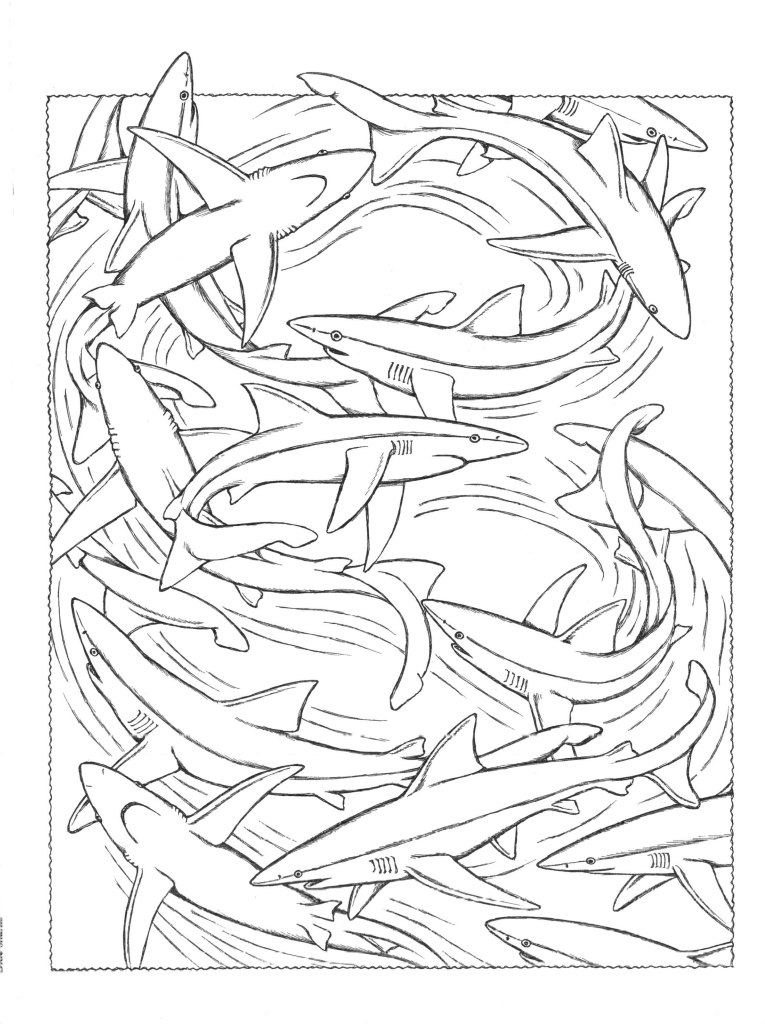

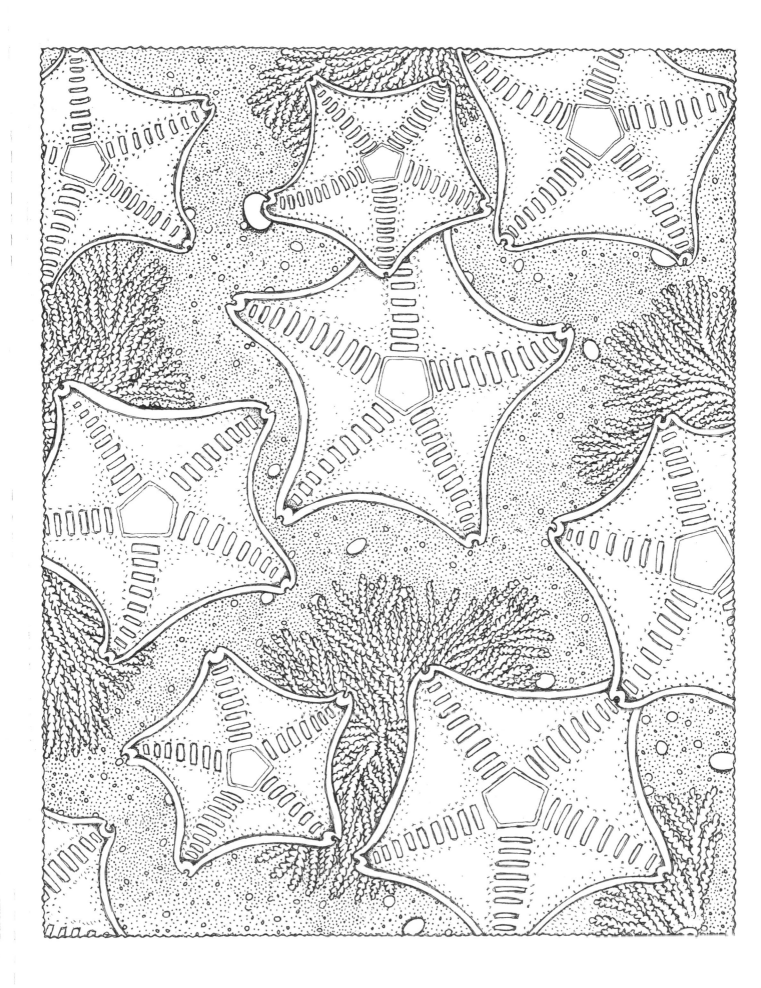

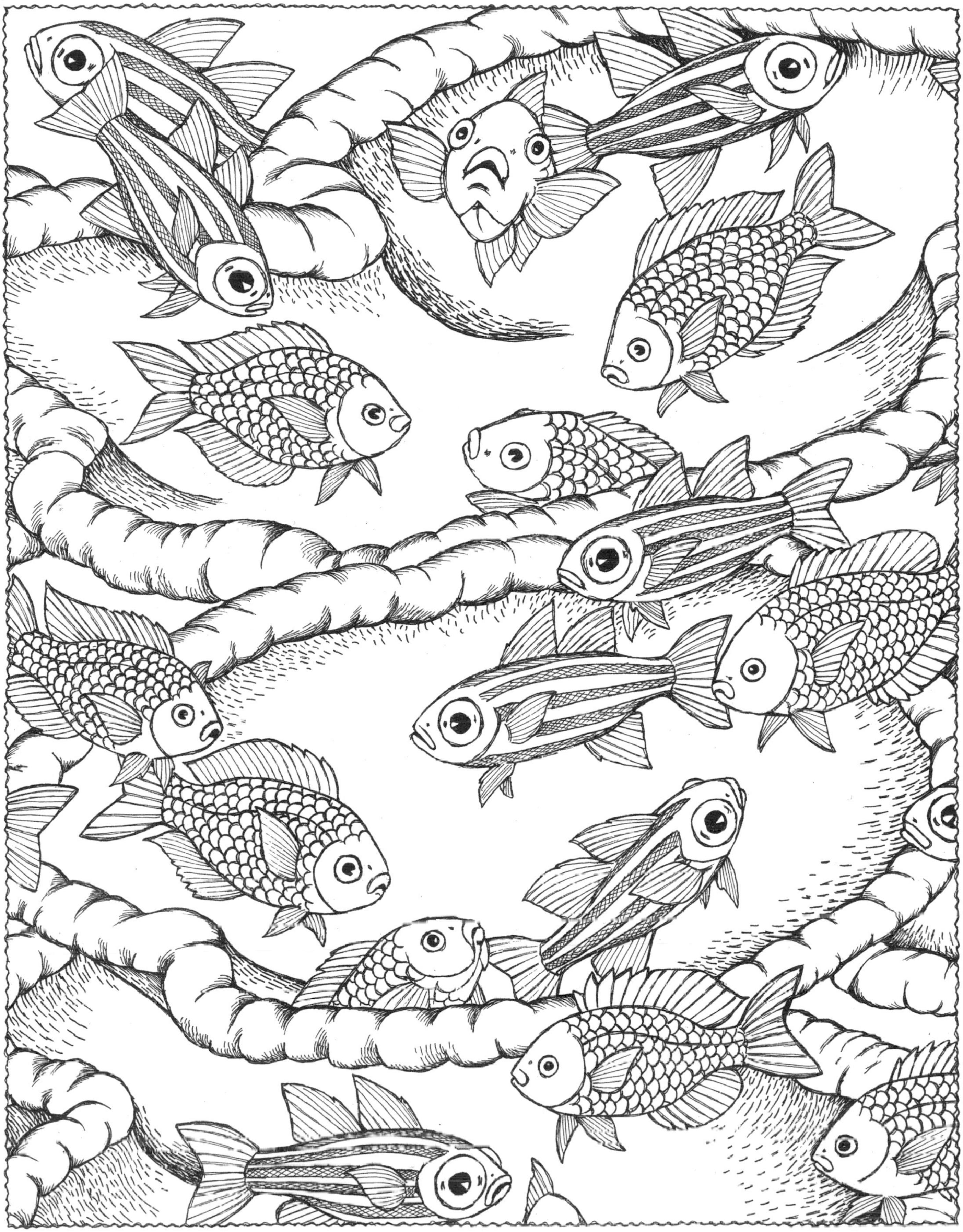

Cardinalfish, damselfish and coral

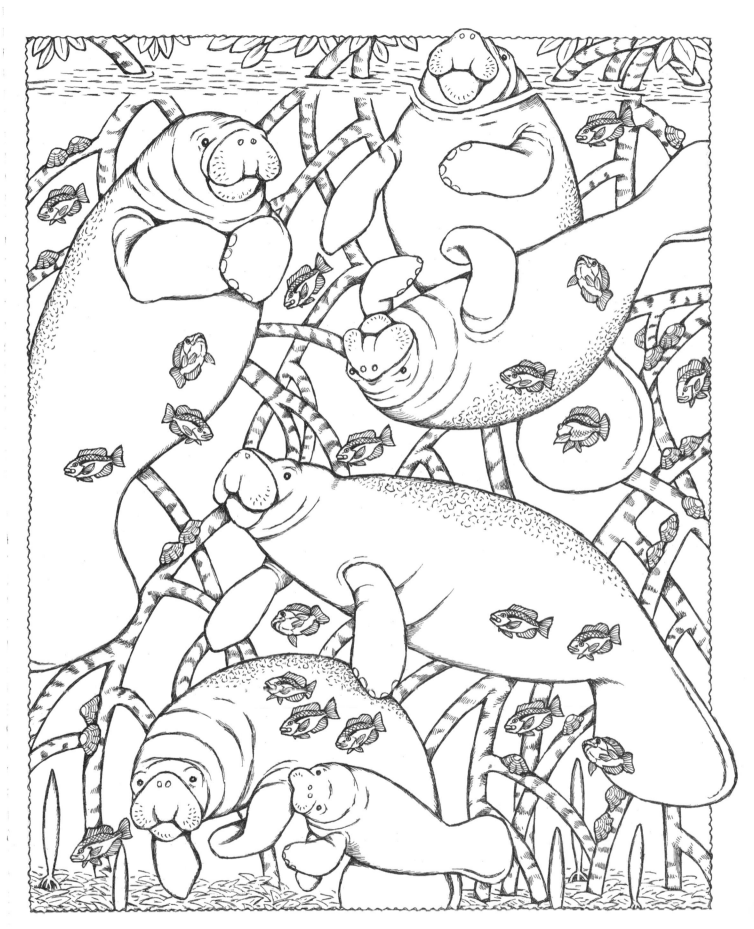

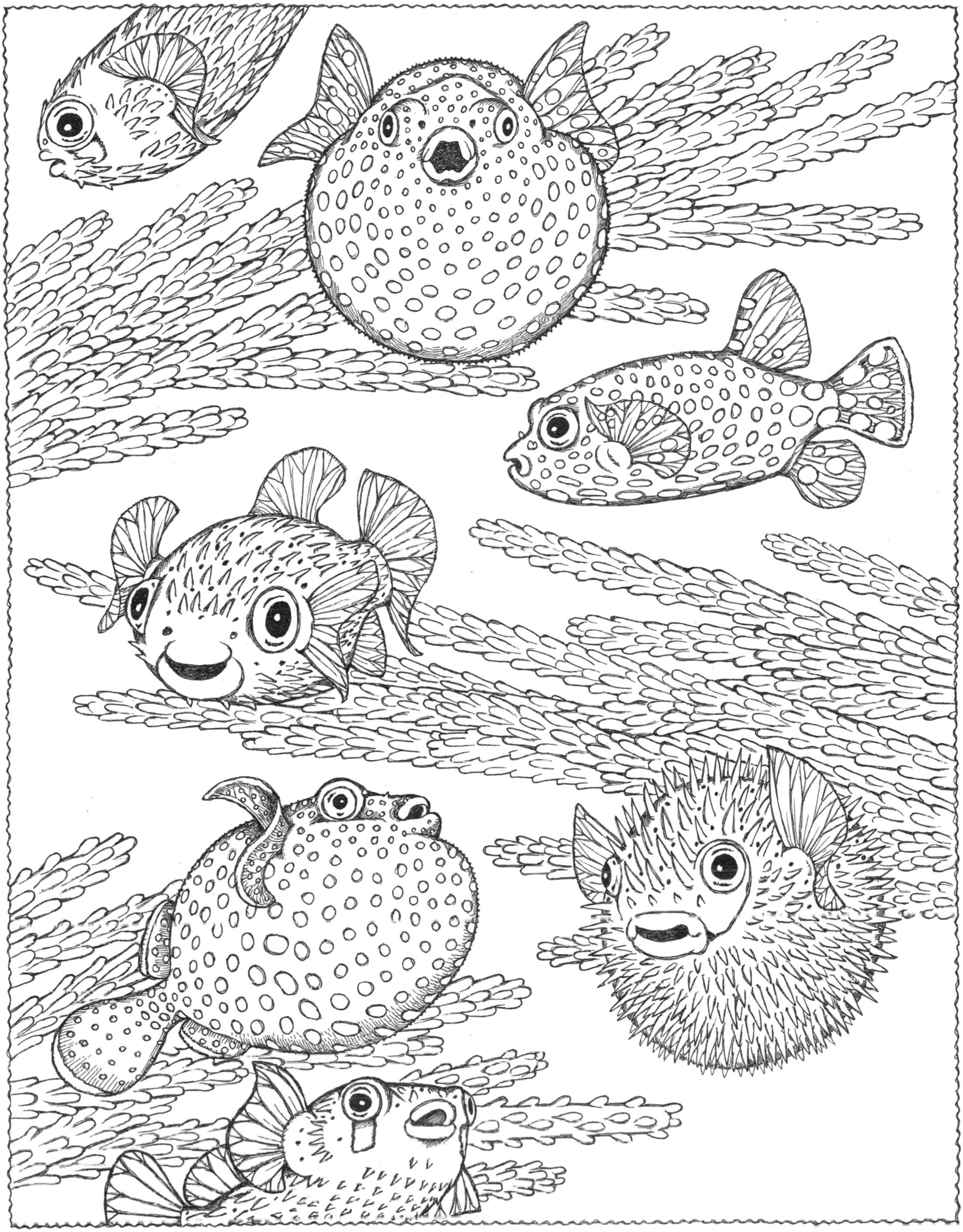

Puffer fish, porcupinefish and whip coral

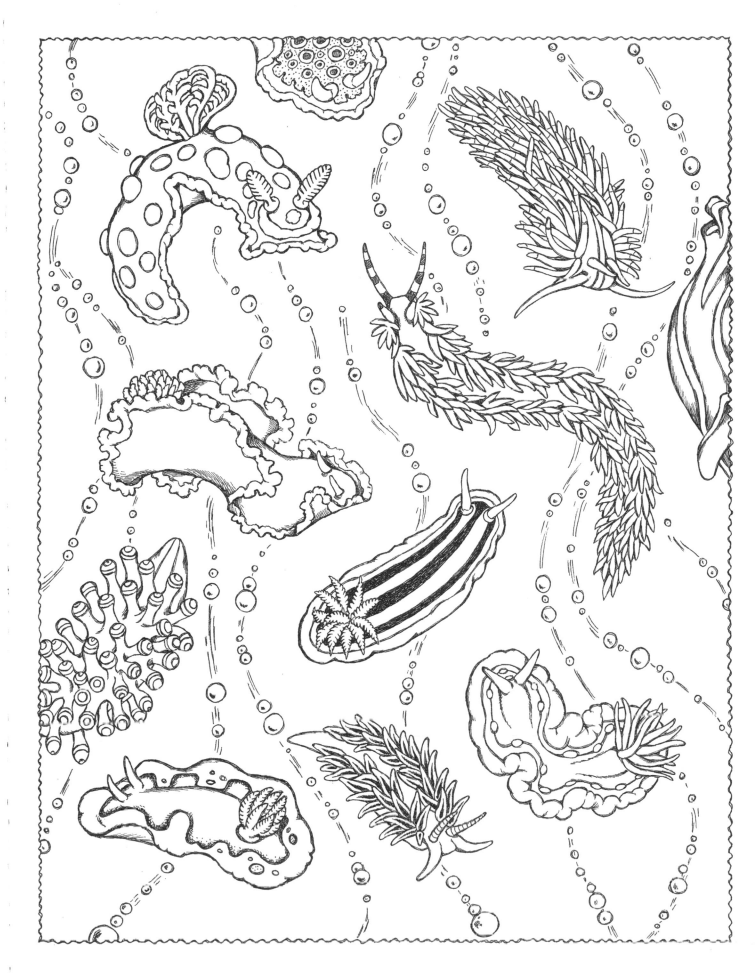

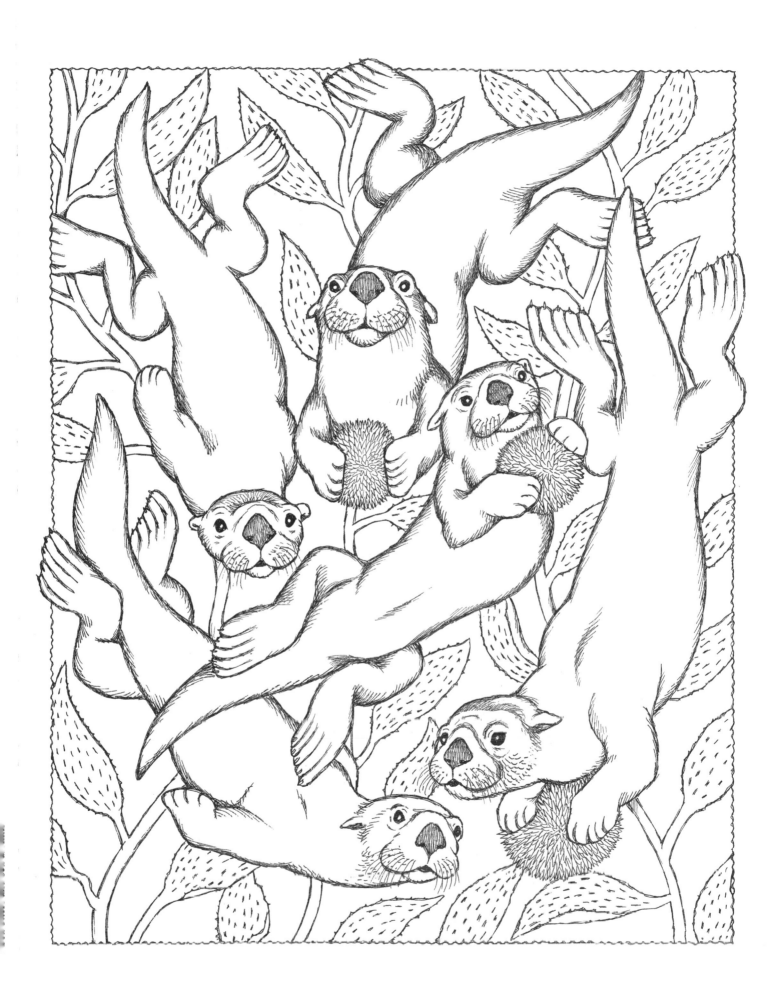

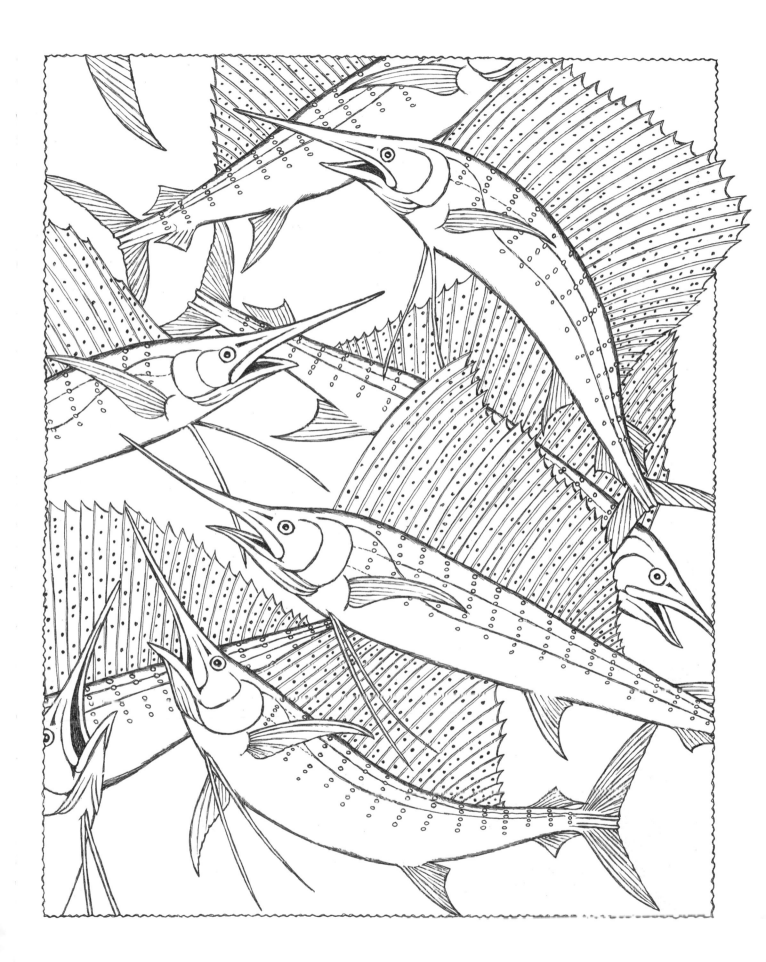

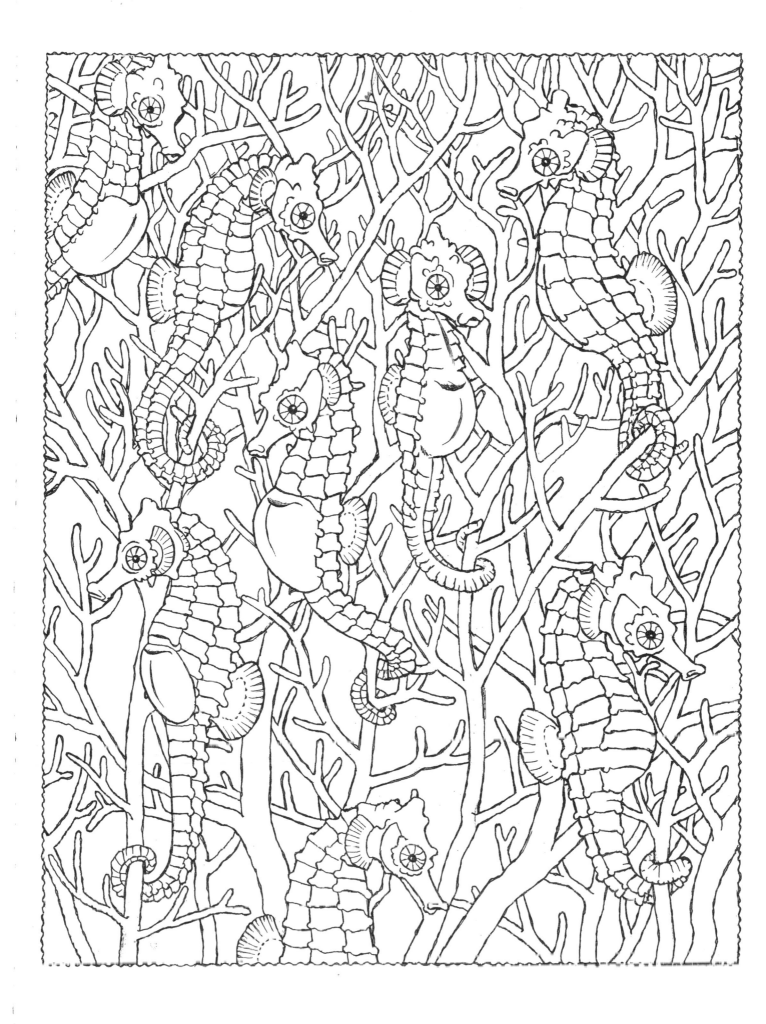

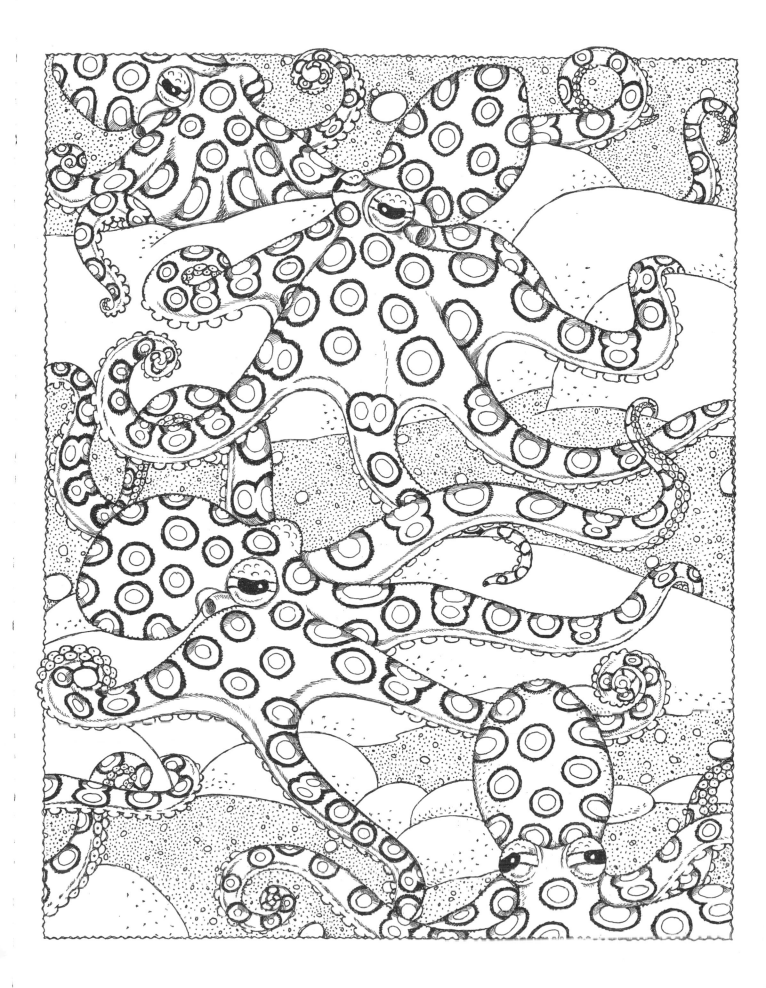

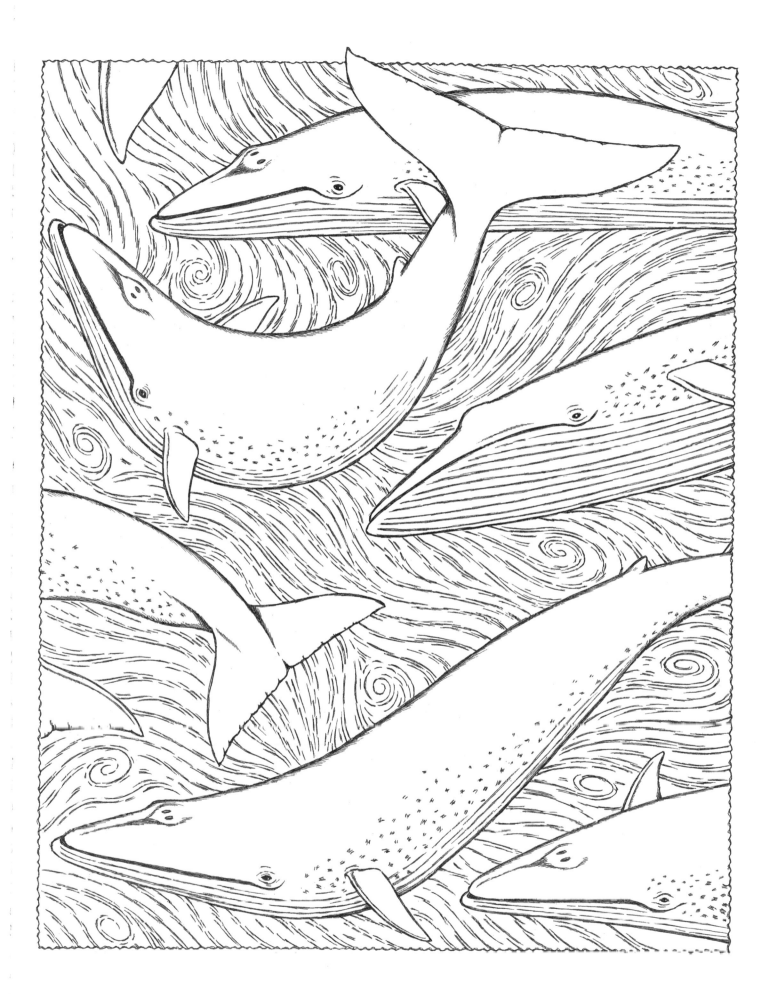

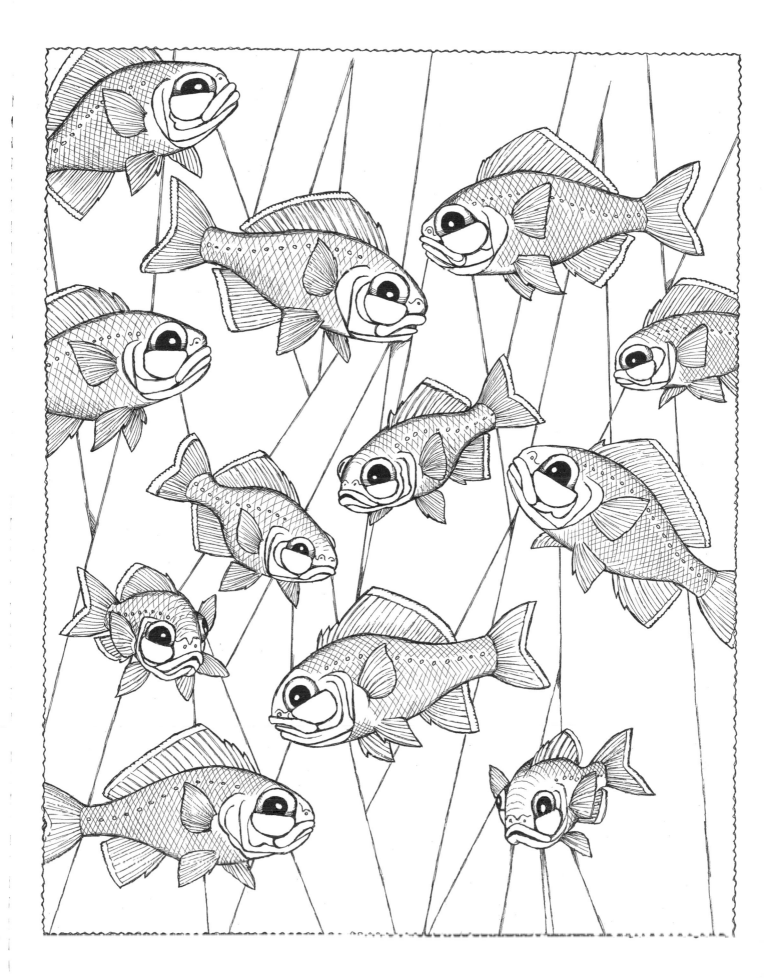

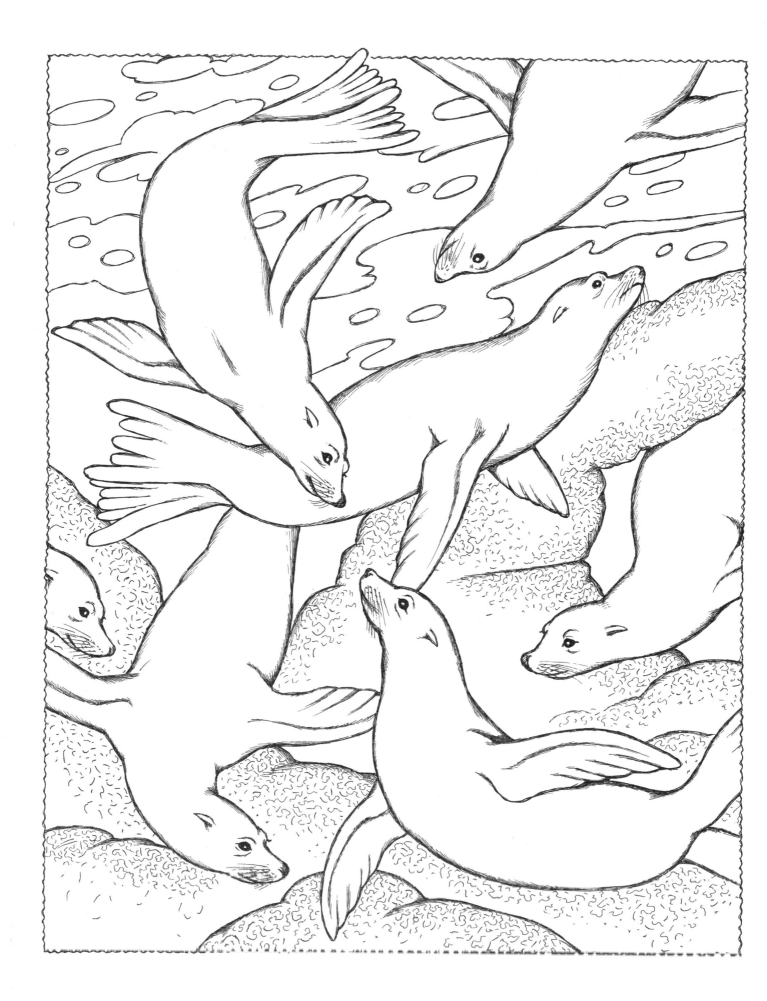

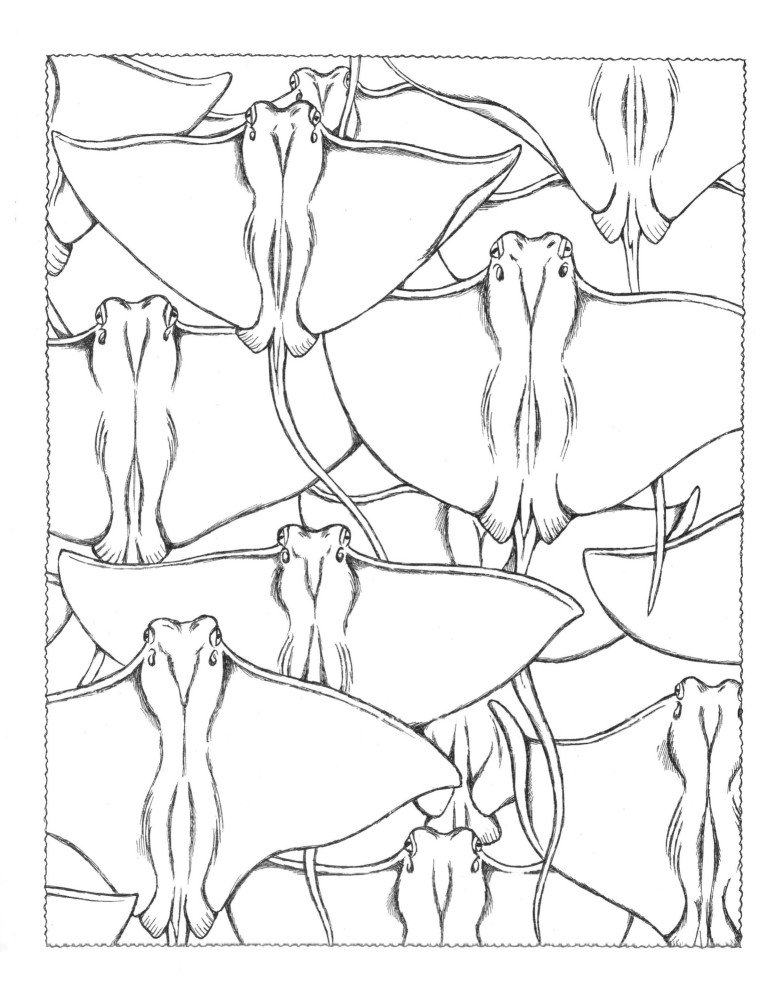

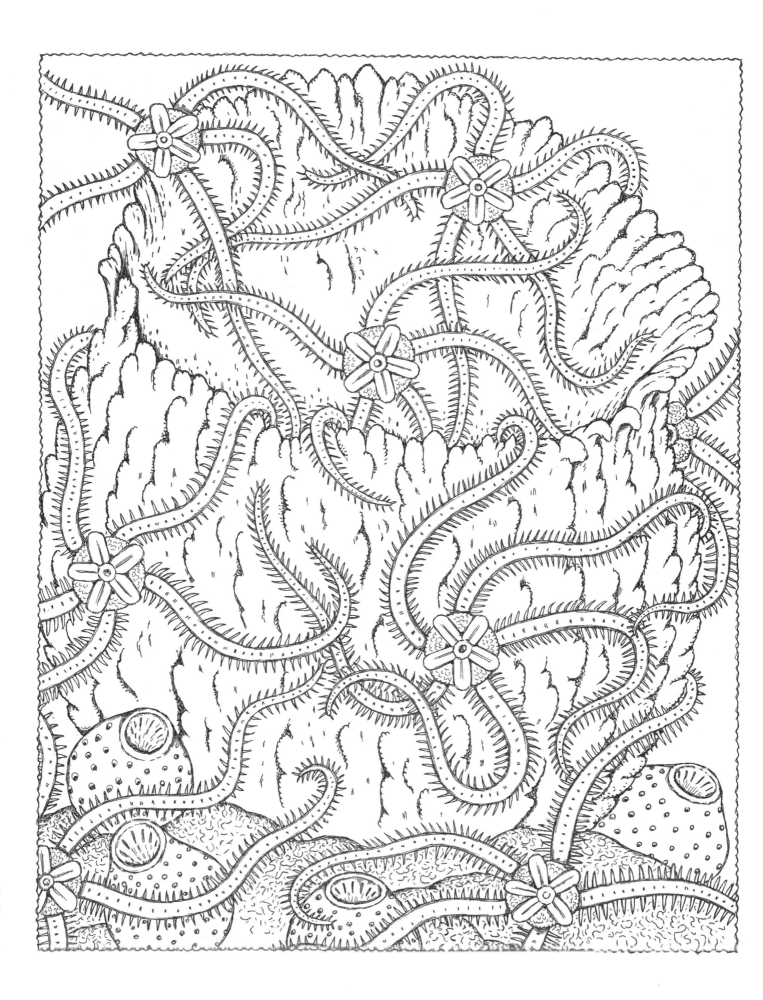

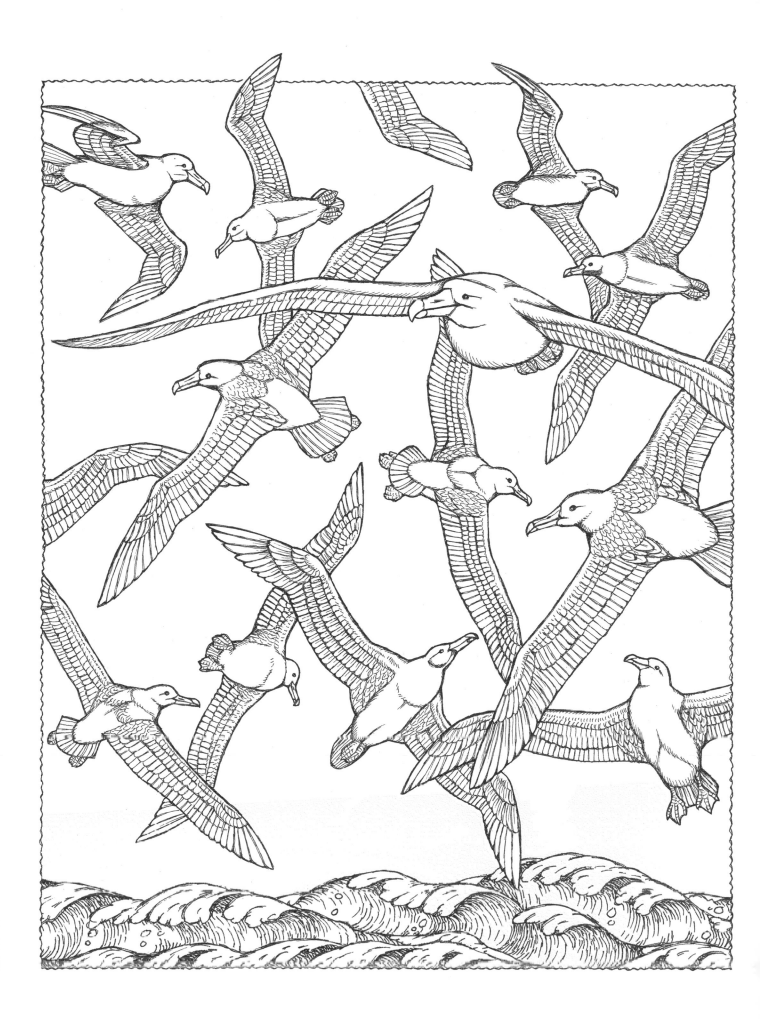

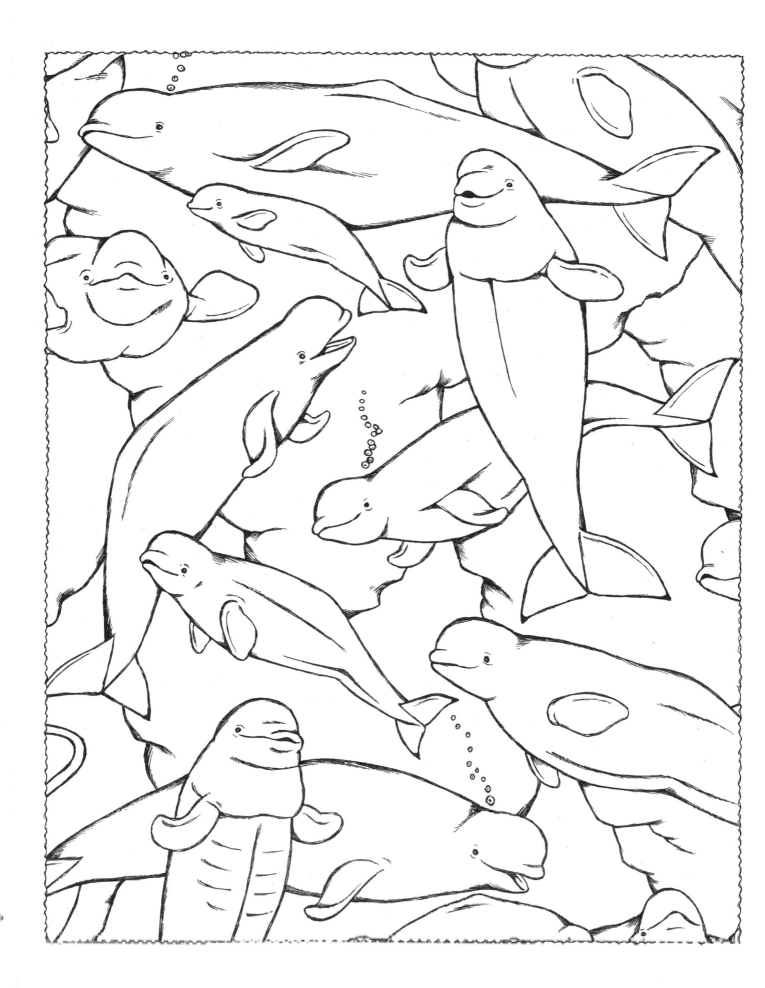

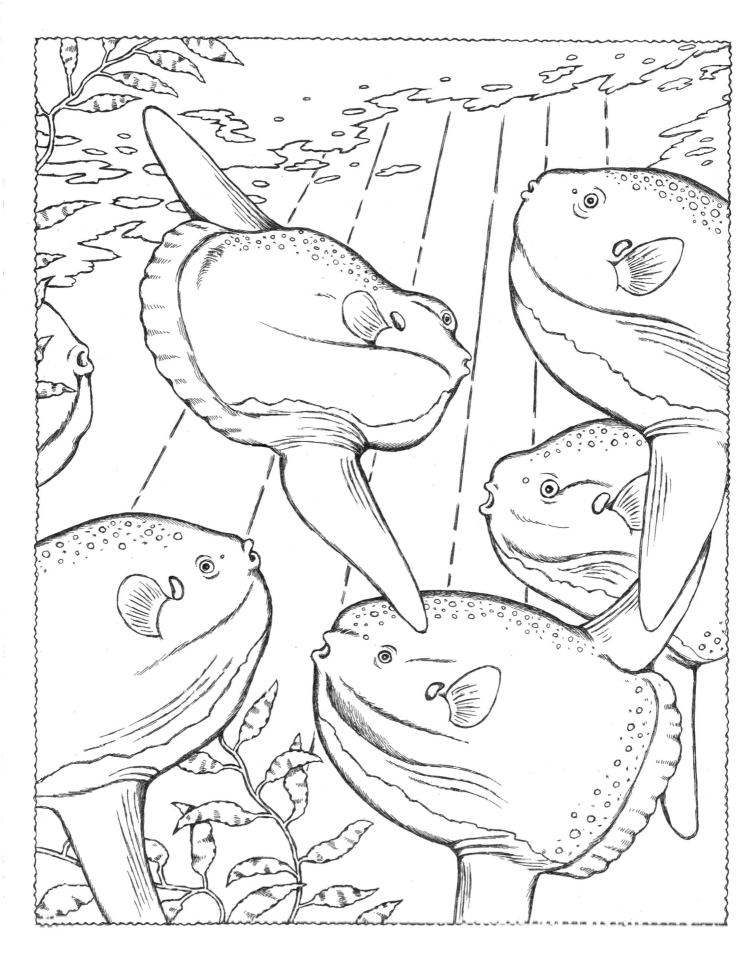

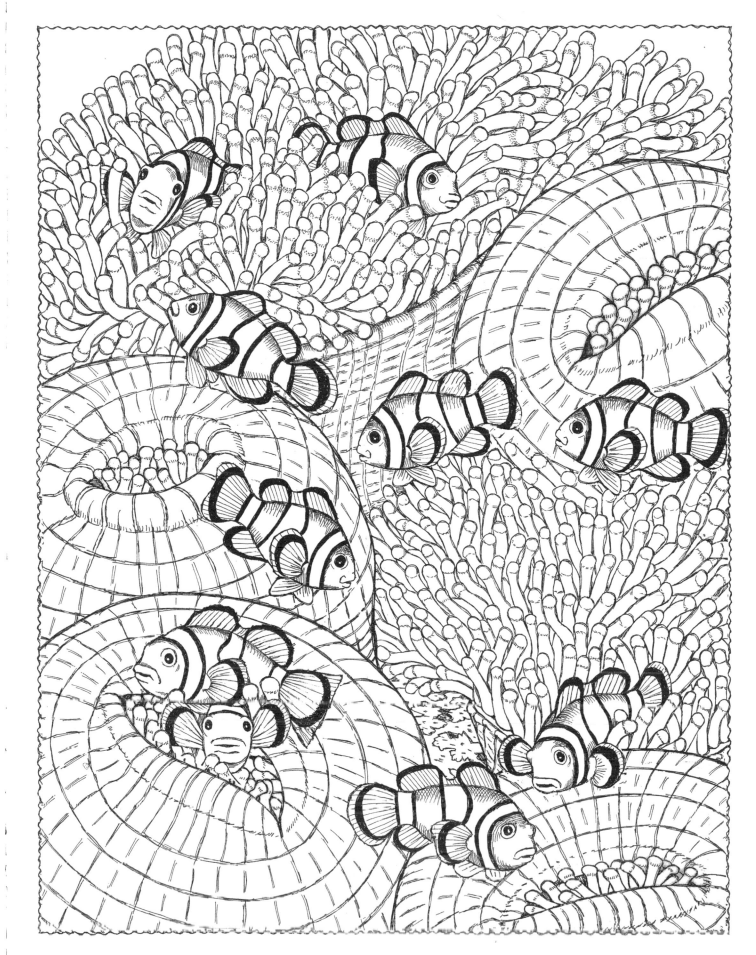

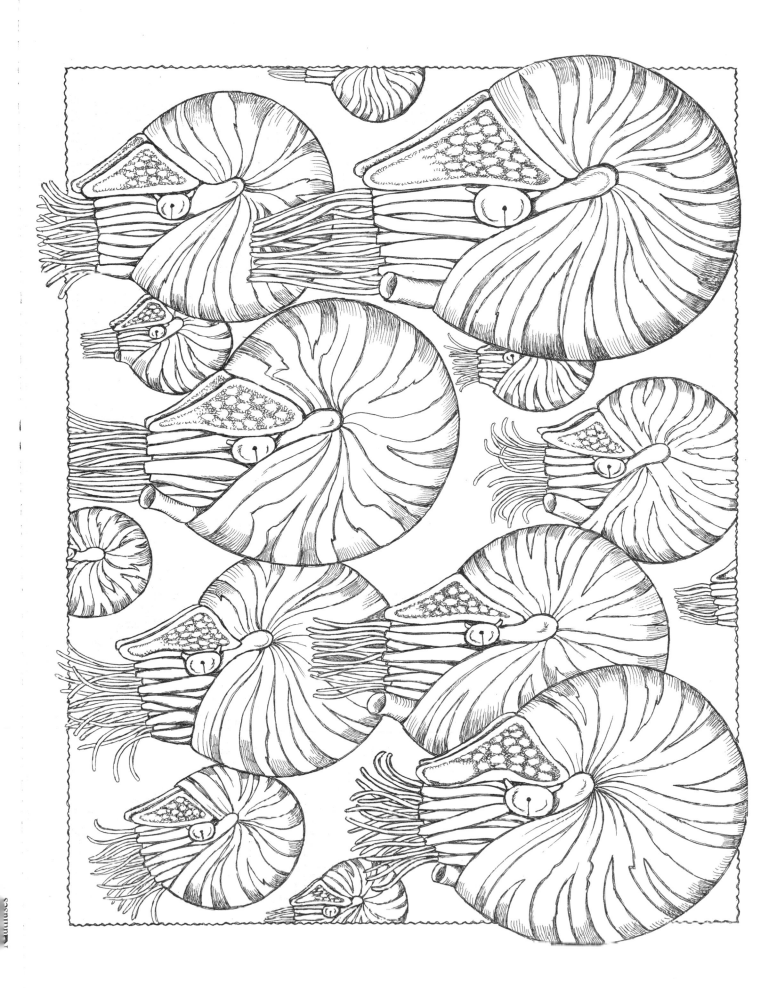

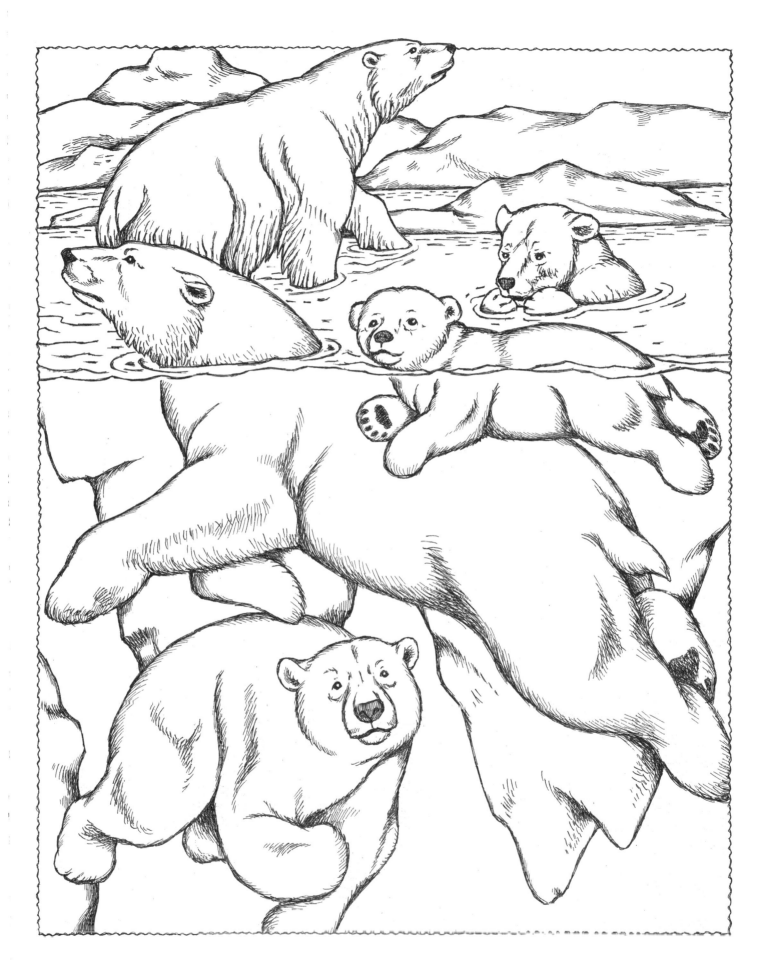

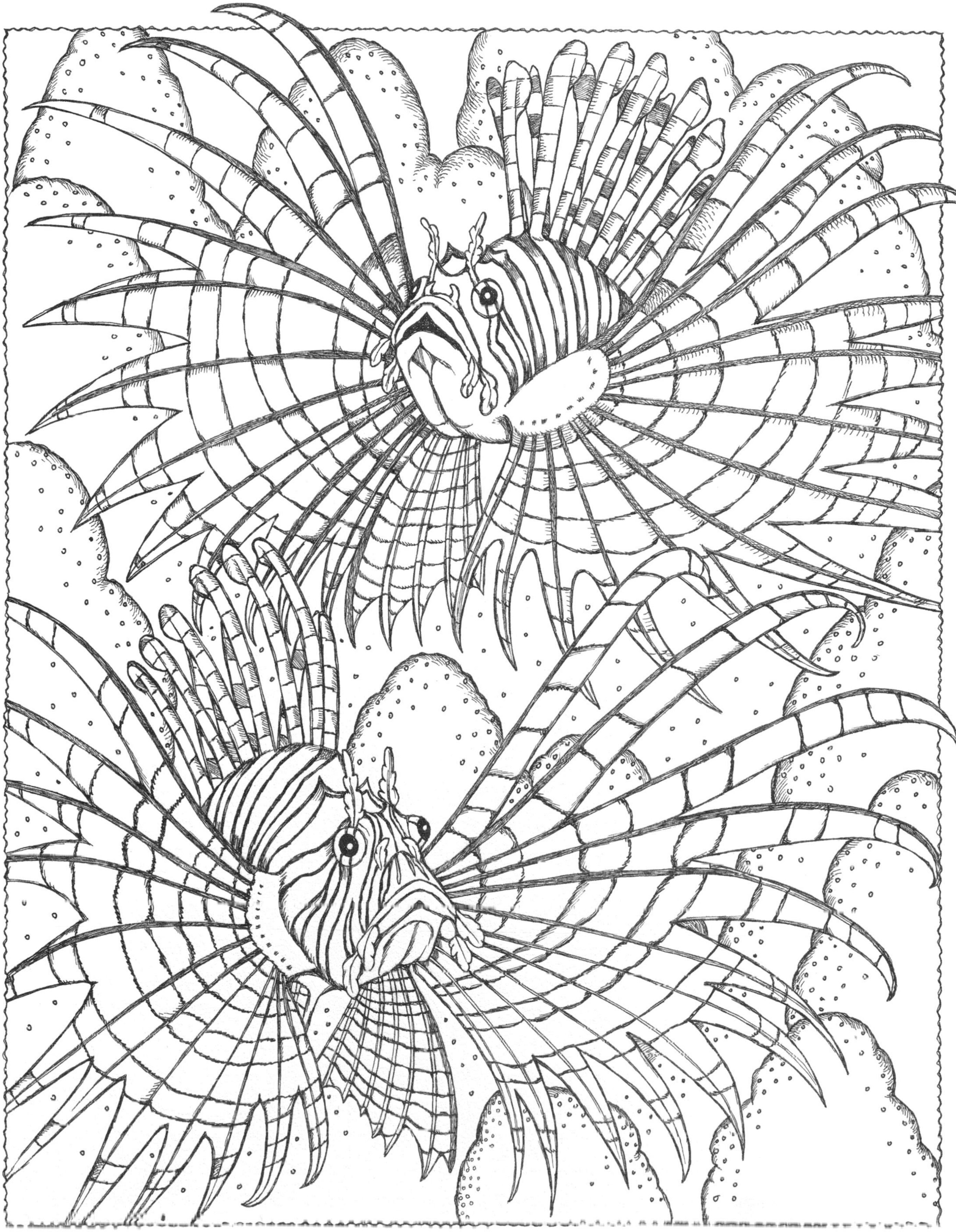

Lionfish and columnar coral

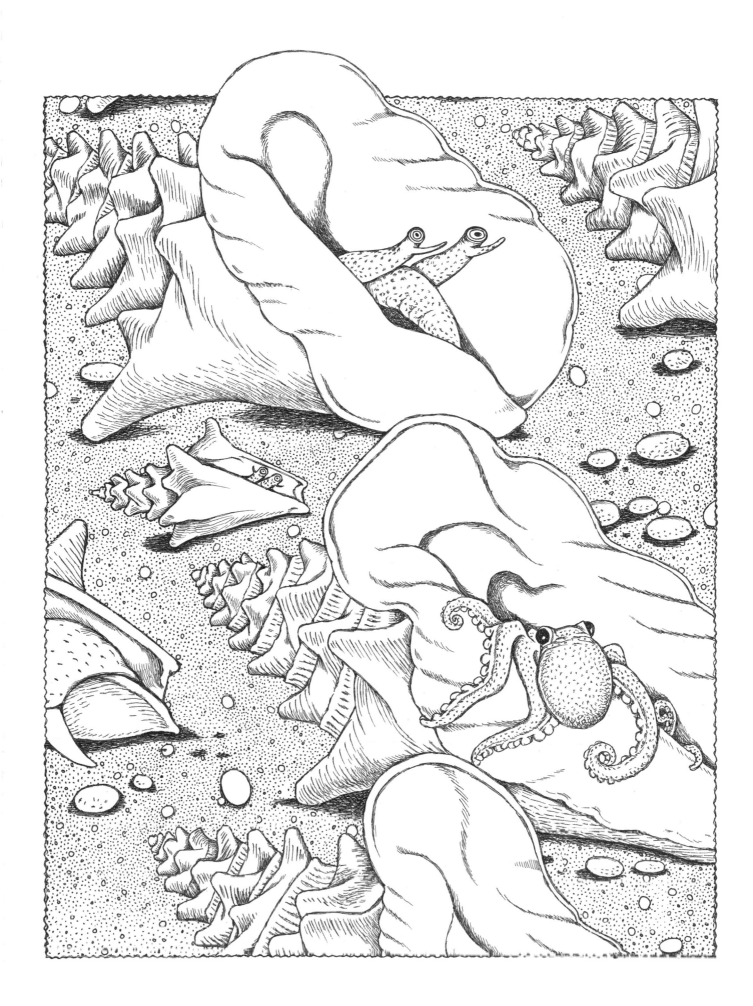

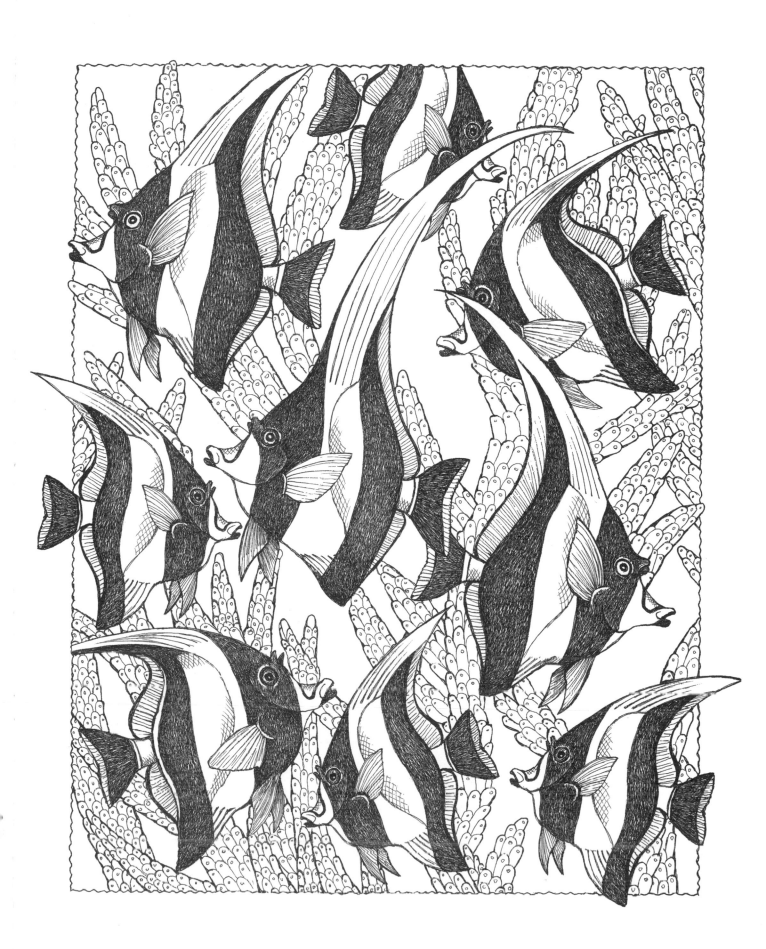

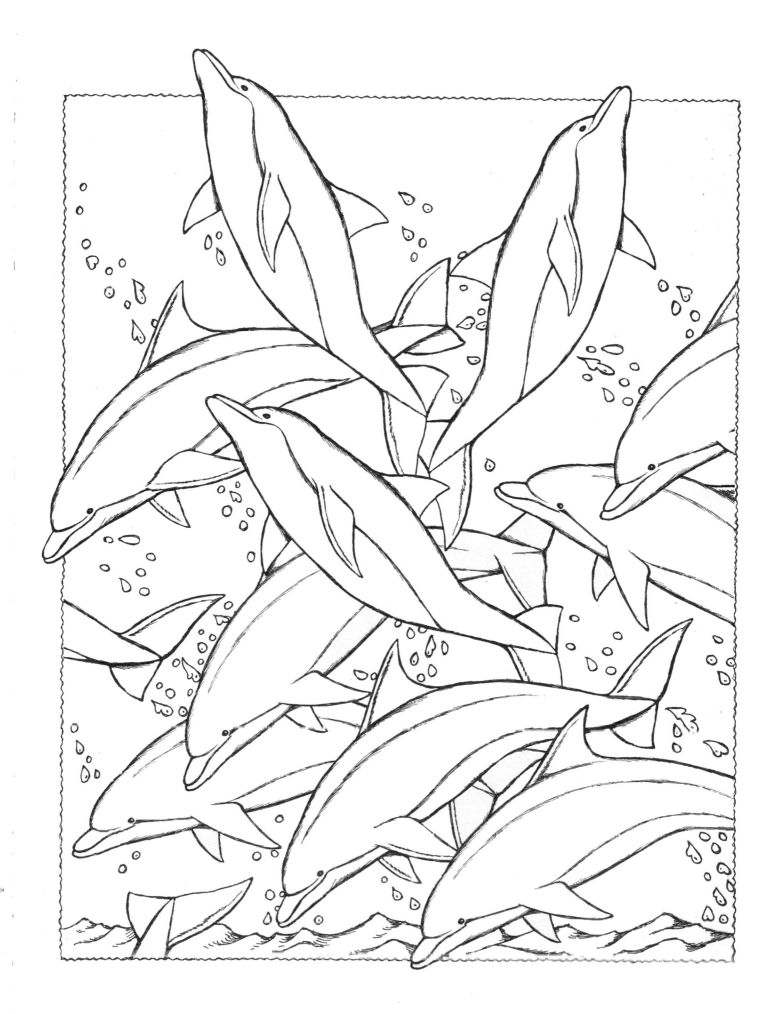

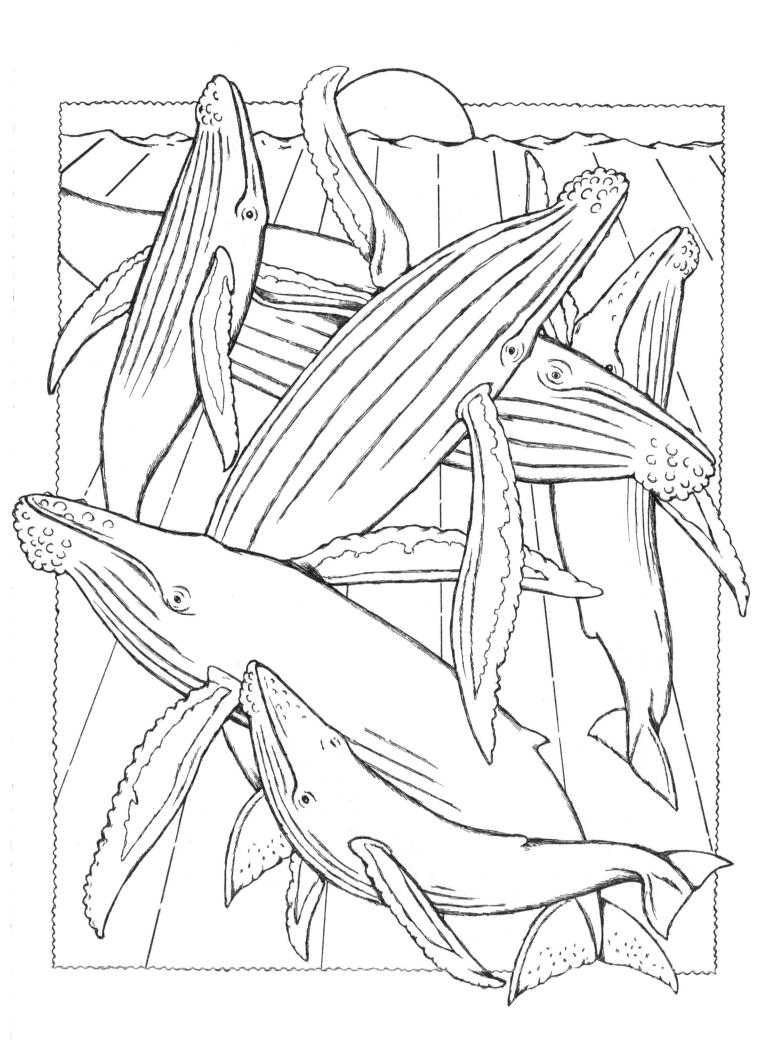

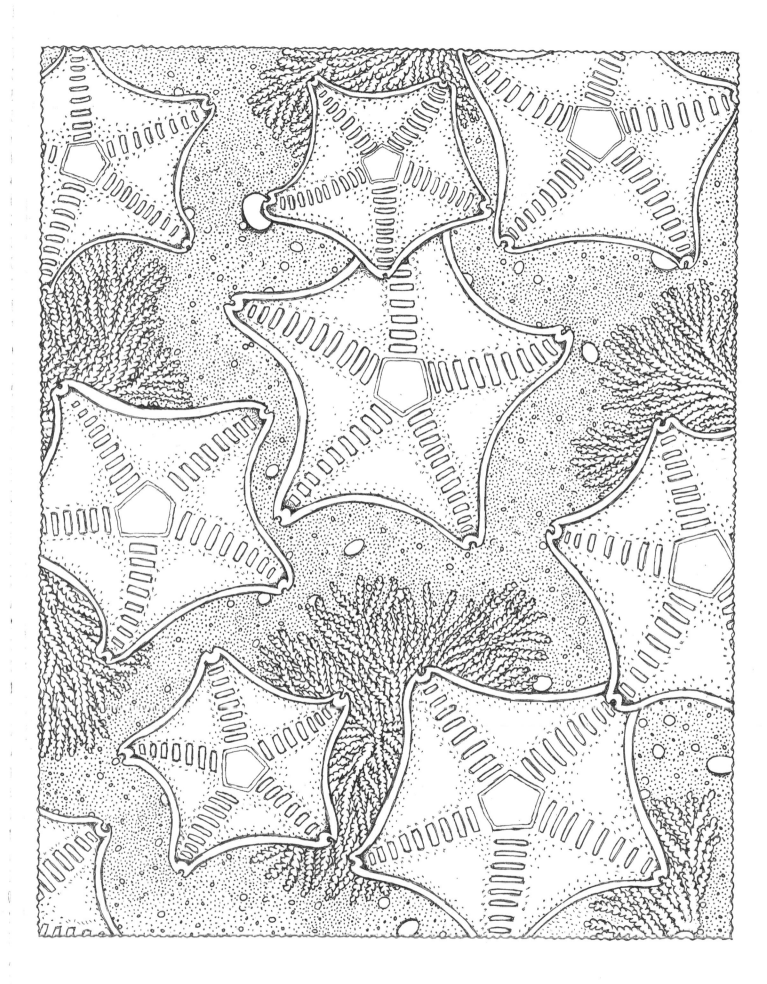